BEING THE CHURCH IN
OCCUPIED TERRITORY

Copyright 2011
by The House Studio and The Work of the People

ISBN 978-0-8341-2595-7

Printed in the United States of America

Cover and Interior Design by Arthur Cherry

thehousestudio.com

10 9 8 7 6 5 4 3 2 1

SUNDAY ASYLUM

BEING THE CHURCH IN
OCCUPIED TERRITORY
STANLEY HAUERWAS
WITH JASON BARNHART

CONTENTS

INTRODUCTION

I had been a Christian for only about two years when I began my freshman year at Ashland University. I felt the call to ministry and knew from day one that I was going to be a Religion major. As college students normally do, I formed friendships, met the faculty of my department, and began the next chapter of my life.

One of my professors was Dr. Kyle Fedler. Kyle was so influential in my life that I cannot share my story without mentioning his name. He challenged me while also unearthing my pride, arrogance, and spiritual superiority. He exposed me to a tragic lack of understanding of this thing we call church.

When I arrived at Ashland, I was a classic evangelical who knew I was saved but had no larger picture or understanding of the church other than it being a place I went on Sundays. Like so many other Christians, I believed God was safe, that he promised us safety. I believed faith was logical certainty and believing the right things. The lived out part of Christianity was separated from the conceptual, intellectual side of Christianity. My head was light years away from my heart.

Perhaps most importantly during my time learning from him,

Kyle introduced me to the writings of two men who forever changed my life and altered my view of Christianity. The first was John Howard Yoder, a theologian from the Mennonite/ Anabaptist perspective. (But to limit Yoder to the Mennonites would be to unfairly pigeonhole the man; he did, after all, teach at the University of Notre Dame, a Catholic school, and his writings were directed many times at evangelicalism in America.) His writings on the alternative community of the church have so shaped my understanding of the church's mission that I don't need to think about "how Yoder would understand the church." His theology just simply flows out of the man I have become and am becoming.

Yoder had a profound influence on the next theologian who altered, really wrecked (in a good way), my life. That man was Stanley Hauerwas. Both Yoder and Hauerwas have always amazed me because they hold out ridiculous hope for this idea called church. Their writings (through Kyle) altered my thinking on Christianity and the church. I began to hope and believe that the church was more than *song, sermon, song.* I began to believe that God wanted to do extraordinary things through the church's witness and had, in fact, already been doing that for millennia (it's called church history).

Church became for me a risky, demanding, frustrating, necessary component of the Christian life. In fact, if I can let you in on a little secret, I don't think we can be Christians without it. The church is the tangible reminder that Christ has a body, that Christ has a mission, and that the two are connected in some bizarre, mystical, adventurous sort of way.

Hauerwas authored a book with William Willimon[1] called *Resident Aliens: Life in the Christian Colony.* In it they detail what I believe to be the mission of the church and to what I've sought to give my life. They write:

> The Gospels make wonderfully clear that the disciples had not the foggiest idea of what they had gotten into when they followed Jesus. With a simple "Follow me," Jesus invited ordinary people to come out and be part of an adventure, a journey that kept surprising them at every turn in the road. It is no coincidence that the Gospel writers chose to frame the gospel in terms of a journey.

> The church exists today as resident aliens, an adventurous colony in a society of unbelief. As a society of unbelief, Western culture is devoid of a sense of journey, of adventure, because it lacks belief in much more than the cultivation of an ever-shrinking horizon of self-preservation and self-expression."[2]

---

[1] William Willimon is Presiding Bishop of the North Alabama Conference of the Methodist Church and Visiting Research Professor at Duke Divinity School in Durham, North Carolina.

[2] Stanley Hauerwas and William Willimon, *Resident Aliens: Life in the Christian Colony* (Nashville: Abingdon Press 1989), 49.

The church exists for adventure, journey, surprise, risk, hope, alternative—as an alien people in the world. We do things differently, live differently, treat people differently, and obey a different code that is foreign and foolish to most of the world. There is something in the witness of the church that speaks to a void in the dominant culture. The church embodies what Jesus said in John 10:10: "The thief comes only to steal and kill and destroy; I have come that they may have life, and have it to the full."

Sunday Asylum is born out of this quest for adventure and risk—*Sunday* symbolizing the day we gather and tell the story again to one another, *Asylum* because the true story at the heart of Christianity is just crazy and we need to get together in a safe place and do a reality check (kingdom/church style) about this mission to which we're called.

Welcome to the adventure that is *Sunday Asylum!*

01

BELIEVE vs. MAKE BELIEVE

Video Transcript—Stanley Hauerwas

I think evangelicalism, which comes very much out of certain reformed theological developments, tends to be very rationalistic. You *believe* stuff. And of course, I think you need to believe stuff, but I'm just not that interested in belief. I mean, I'm a very orthodox Christian, I hope, and I affirm Nicaea and Chalcedon. I believe Scripture is the word of God and so on.

VIDEO TRANSCRIPT

And I want to believe whatever the church tells me to believe. But I think belief as *the* indicator of what makes one a Christian tends to separate the work of the language of the faith from its work. What is it doing? And I'm much more interested in trying to locate the context in which the language does the work that it never occurs to me to say, well do I believe that?

I mean, I think of it as laying brick. Bricklayers, people love to watch bricklayers because they can't quite figure out how it's being done. When a bricklayer cuts the mud off the board and spreads it done the course, people oftentimes don't notice that they will then take their trowel and frog the mud. Froggin' the mud makes a trench down the mud they just spread. It not only puts the mud out toward the edge of the brick, where you'll get a joint, but when you frog the mud, that creates a vacuum. A good bricklayer almost never touches the brick with their trowel because they just let the vacuum pull the brick down to being true to the line.

That's the way I wanna think about theological speech. Most people wouldn't know what you're talking about when you talk about froggin' the mud. So you talk about what it means to worship Jesus as the second person of the trinity in the context in which you're froggin' mud. I mean it's doing work. And that's the way I tend to think about it. Namely, it's not isolatable beliefs, it's doing work.

Should we learn how to lay bricks again? Have we forgotten how to be human?

Absolutely. I think you tend to forget what it means to be human all the time. And it is a training. Training is very much at the heart of Christianity for me. It's an ongoing process of learning, of being trained to do work that is inseparable from the training, so in the process of the training you become transformed in ways that you hardly notice you're being transformed in order to be able to do the work that needs to be done.

DISCUSSION QUESTIONS

What does Hauerwas mean when he says, "I want to believe whatever the church tells me to?" Is it simply buying everything the church says without evaluating the information? Why or why not?

Do you agree that the "work of the language of the faith" has been separated from the work of the faith? What has this looked like in the church?

How do you respond to Hauerwas saying, "I'm just not that interested in belief?" What do you think he means?

What does it mean to forget we are human? Do you agree that we sometimes forget what it means to be human? How? How can we begin to remember what it means to be human?

Belief as *the* indicator of what makes one a Christian tends to separate the work of the language of the faith from its work.

STANLEY HAUERWAS

Faith in God, then, is not at all the same as the kind of logical certainty that we attain in Euclidean geometry. God is not the conclusion to a process of reasoning, the solution to a mathematical problem. To believe in God is not to accept the possibility of his existence because it has been "proved" to us by some theoretical argument, but it is to put our trust in One whom we know and love. Faith is not the supposition that something might be true, but the assurance that someone is there.[3]

BISHOP KALLISTOS WARE

[3] Bishop Kallistos Ware, *The Orthodox Way* (Crestwood, NY: St. Vladimir's Seminary Press 1979), 14.

I remember my years in seminary fondly. Seminary was a time of great challenge and growth for me. As I reflect back on those years, I realize that one particular area of growth for me came through exposure to different perspectives—not just from

COMMENTARY

faculty but also from my colleagues. In a single classroom one could encounter fifteen different "brands" of Christianity. Because of these different perspectives there always seemed to be some disagreement and misunderstanding. The everlasting question I had was, "How can two people read the same thing and come to completely different conclusions?" (Bear in mind I'm not talking about orthodoxy versus heresy here but differing ideas of application.)

One day it dawned on me. The tension in the room was in regards to differences in lived theology. The academic theology of textbooks remained the same, but the application of the information gathered was very different. Although we all loved studying the church, a Caucasian, middle-class Presbyterian saw church differently than an African-American, upper-class Baptist did. We both affirmed the importance of the church, but the fleshing out of such an idea was incredibly diverse.

And at the same time, even though the incarnation (the fleshing out) of those ideas looked different, there was still an eerie similarity to all the viewpoints. It wasn't that everyone applied the ideas in the same way. The similarity came in that every student felt the ideas *needed to be applied*. So even in great diversity, we still felt and experienced unity.

All brands of Western Christianity have their own peculiar characteristics. The Enlightenment has attempted to get us to buy into this idea that the divine world is separate from the material, earthly world. Our business in the here and now is to get busy living out our own life and our own story.

American Christianity has been heavily influenced by this ideology. From many of the country's Founding Fathers to the present, American Christianity has been much more comfortable with a deistic approach to God (namely that God created the world and stepped back from it) than with a theistic God (a God who is actively involved and engaged with his created world). For much of American Christian expression, Jesus has been all about making good, moral people whose only means of religious transcendence (experiencing something beyond themselves) is a reduced, therapeutic understanding of prayer—"God, I want" or "God, help me."

Therefore, a classic American theological attribute is separating theology (what we believe) from ethics (how we behave). Theology becomes a textbook journey, and lived theology becomes a behavior of maniacs. It seems that Western

Christianity, which is extremely rationalistic and individualistic, has been the victor. So we get a lot of good, moral believers who have no understanding of larger issues of justice in the world. Faith is a concept, and discipleship is a long list of memorization rather than the creation of a peculiar people on mission for a peculiar God.

Something has gone desperately wrong.

This is what Hauerwas is speaking to in this video. The work of the language of the faith, the orthodox theological truths, has been separated from the actual work itself. We fall victim to the lie that what we believe doesn't necessarily shape how we behave. The heart of true theology, however, is that our God is not a concept but a person. The gospel is Jesus Christ himself. In Jesus we see the union of orthodoxy and behavior. The central Christian message is that God came in the flesh. Our central theological concept is at the same time a central theological action. In Jesus, belief and action are tied together. Read these words from John's Gospel:

> In the beginning was the Word, and the Word was with God, and the Word was God (1:1). The Word became flesh and made his dwelling among us. We have seen his glory, the glory of the One and Only, who came from the Father, full of grace and truth (1:14).

In the incarnation (God in the flesh) we see a God who takes great theological action, but we also see a God who takes on the flesh to show us what it means to be fully human; Jesus is said to be fully God and fully human—the Word took on flesh and dwelled among us. This is at the heart of Christianity. God does not speak against the material world and elevate some enlightened spiritual world. In Jesus, God fully affirmed that the material world matters. As a result then, the follower of Jesus is the embodiment of the spoken Word of God on mission for God.

For the Christian, Hauerwas would say, discipleship is the ongoing process of being trained and transformed by community into greater Christlikeness. If we separate the language of the faith from the work, we miss this valuable truth. Thus, when we separate belief from work, we create a dualistic world in which what we believe is different from how we behave.

In his letter to the church in Ephesus, Paul states a very bold truth when he writes:

> With all wisdom and understanding, [God] made known to us the mystery of his will according to his good pleasure, which he purposed in Christ, to be put into effect when the times have reached their fulfillment—to bring all things in heaven and on earth together under one head, even Christ. (Eph. 1:8b-10)

The Greco-Roman world of Paul, out of which much of Western thought has been shaped, also sought to separate language from work. The mystery is that Jesus is available to all, even Gentiles. In Jesus, Paul is saying, heaven and earth have come together. They are unified; they are made one. No matter how far the Enlightenment and our modernized world seek to separate the two, they cannot override this overarching truth. And our language of the faith, because of this divine act, cannot be separated from the work of the faith.

When the world looks at followers of Jesus, they should see a masterpiece of what it means to be a people fully alive, fully present, and fully confident in their Lord. We are the result of God's activity. We are a people of life in a world of death. Just as God spoke the world into existence and the creation happened, so also followers of Jesus live their theology in such a way that their witness (language and work) creates an alternative reality to the ways of the world in which they find themselves.

Followers of Jesus recognize their citizenship is with and in the kingdom of God. And what Hauerwas is attempting to get across to his audience is that the church cannot separate language and work because the language makes sense only in the context of a believing community manifesting (read "working" in) an alternative reality.

So sitting in that seminary classroom, I've come to realize, was a modern day parable of this important truth. Theology and ethics separate is foolishness. Practical theology is also kind of a misnomer. All theology is practical and longs to be applied. The particular speech acts of Christians manifest an alternative reality that doesn't just take souls to heaven—it looks at people and shows them how to be fully human again.

DISCUSSION QUESTIONS

Do you see a difference between "academic theology" and "lived theology?" If so, how?

Respond to the statement, "all theology is practical and longs to be applied." Do you agree? Why or why not?

What might a Christian life look like that "doesn't just take souls to heaven" but "looks at people and shows them how to be fully human again?" How does this kind of Christianity change our responsibility to those around us?

02

CONFLICT vs. COMFORT

Video Transcript—Stanley Hauerwas

> **I think "community" is getting to the point in the church that the word "love" has, that it's overused.**

VIDEO TRANSCRIPT

I'd talk about church. It's a pretty good word. The problem with "community" is people associate it with people that like one another, and of course good communities are spaces where people love one another enough that they're not afraid of disagreements and the kinds of conflicts necessary for the discovery of the goods that otherwise could not be discovered if you weren't in conflict with one another. And so how to get a sense of the necessity of people sharing a history sufficient to provide arguments, I mean that's called church history, and it's hard to recover. And you don't get it just by the word "community."

People that are together to be together, that's just another name for hell, as Sartre well understood. I mean, you never are to gather to be together. You're to gather because you have something you want to do, and to work. And so, we worship God. I just think that's a bottom line that has to be there that people have work to do together.

I'm kind of in mourning. My rector, as I said, this last Sunday was his last Sunday, yesterday. And Timothy, in addressing the congregation between services, said, "Now you all, some people have expressed worry about staying together." He said, "if you think your project is to stay together, you're doomed. Your project is to witness to the cross and everything depends on that. Do that and you won't have to worry about staying together." That's a word that seems to me to be true.

DISCUSSION QUESTIONS

Think again about Hauerwas's statement that as Christians we're "never to gather to be together. [We're] to gather because [we] have something [we] want to do, and to work." Do you agree with this statement? Why or why not?

How does the church "witness to the cross?"

What does true community look like? Have you experienced it?

What does it mean for a people to "share a history?"

The problem with "community" is
people associate it with people
that like one another.

STANLEY HAUERWAS

By sheer grace, God will not permit us to live even for a brief period in a dream world. He does not abandon us to those rapturous experiences and lofty moods that come over us like a dream. God is not a God of the emotions but the God of truth. Only that fellowship which faces such disillusionment, with all its unhappy and ugly aspects, begins to be what it should be in God's sight, begins to grasp in faith the promise that is given to it. The sooner this shock of disillusionment comes to an individual and to a community the better for both. A community which cannot bear and cannot survive such a crisis, which insists upon keeping its illusion when it should be shattered, permanently loses in the moment the promise of Christian community. Sooner or later it will collapse. Every human wish dream that is injected into the Christian community is a hindrance to genuine community and must be banished if genuine community is to survive. He who loves his dream of a community more than the Christian community itself becomes a destroyer of the latter, even though his personal intentions may be ever so honest and earnest and sacrificial.[4]

DIETRICH BONHOEFFER

[4] Dietrich Bonhoeffer, *Life Together: The Classic Exploration of Faith in Community* (San Francisco: Harper San Francisco 1954), 14-15.

Marriage is an interesting journey. For those of you who aren't married, you may one day know what I'm talking about. No matter how you look at it, marriage is a beautiful journey, a lifelong adventure. But it isn't all roses and butterflies. At times, it is also one of life's most challenging relationships.

COMMENTARY

This is what Hauerwas is discussing in this video clip when he says, "The problem with 'community' is people associate it with people that like one another." I do, of course, like (love) my wife, but as with any other marriage, we don't always agree. In this way, marriage and the church have much in common.

In reality, a place where everyone likes one another and never disagrees is not true community. It is merely an illusion of community. Just as magnets of similar polarity repel each another, so also community cannot exist when everyone agrees all the time and conflict is absent. What makes true community is the ability to disagree and still belong.

The Apostle Paul captures this when he writes to the church in Corinth:

Now the body is not made up of one part but of many. If

the foot should say, "Because I am not a hand, I do not belong to the body," it would not for that reason cease to be part of the body. And if the ear should say, "Because I am not an eye, I do not belong to the body," it would not for that reason cease to be part of the body. If the whole body were an eye, where would the sense of hearing be? If the whole body were an ear, where would the sense of smell be? But in fact God has arranged the parts in the body, every one of them, just as he wanted them to be. If they were all one part, where would the body be? As it is, there are many parts, but one body. (1 Cor. 12:14-20)

Paul is detailing a mystical phenomenon that occurs within the church. The church is not just an organization or some archaic institution—when the church gathers, it manifests the tangible body of Jesus Christ. But within this body there are tensions. The eyes don't have the same perspective as the feet. The hands do not have the same role as the heart. This tension of differences is what makes the physical body function so perfectly.

This same rule applies to the body of Christ, the church; our differences lead to the unity that is the church. True community allows people to disagree because true community is based in love. If we love only those who are like us, is that really love? In the same way, when we seek to find love by making sure people do everything we want, love ceases being love and becomes lust. By openly disagreeing, people allow others to truly be themselves. A people open enough to share conflict end up sharing a history together. A history creates a legacy, and a legacy is the only thing a people can leave behind when they're long gone.

In the end, we're never really to gather simply to be together. There is a reason why being with my family is different from being with strangers or even coworkers. There is something unique toward which my family is working—namely, being a family—that I do not share with strangers in aisle six of the grocery store or people with whom I spend forty hours a week. Likewise, the church's job is not simply to stay together, but this is often where the church gets held up. We sometimes get so focused on being comfortable that we become complacent. This tendency to drift toward complacency is the biggest enemy of community. True community has a mission that is shared together.

In art and design we are always drawn to what the artist or designer has created. We admire the colors, shapes and textures. What we fail to recognize many times is that an artist is utilizing negative space just as much as the space filled with color and shapes. Negative space is the area intentionally not used. It is the white left on a canvas. Companies like Apple and Google have mastered the art of negative space. When you see Google's main page or look at Apple's logo design, you get the feel of clean simplicity and efficiency. This is all communicated by their use of negative space.

For the church, true community is, as Hauerwas states, to witness to the cross and to the alternative community that is this ragamuffin group of Jesus followers. We have a specific mission to which we're called. The primary task of the church is to be the church. It also means that there will be some along the way who want to avoid the conflict of this journey, to seek to eliminate the negative space. But the church is not called to a good, mediocre journey absent of challenge and conflict and filled with busy work. It is called to greatness because the God we serve is a great God. To be a part of the church is to be a part of a great adventure moving in a particular direction.

Churches that move from good to great are able to subtract good things to pour their limited amounts of time and energy into the great. It's easy to remove bad things from our lives. (I say easy in that it's simple to identify bad behaviors.) It's difficult to take something that is profitable and do away with it. True community has the necessary, hard conversations that help each member remain accountable to the mission and to grow in their relationship with Christ. If we're consumed with simply staying together we'll take the easiest path, reducing community to so much less than it was intended to be.

This all comes full circle to my initial comments on marriage.

Whenever I offer pre-marital counseling to a couple I give them this important reminder: "Community lies on the other side of conflict." A healthy marriage is not one in which the husband and wife never argue. It is not one in which the husband and wife become more like each other. Rather, a healthy marriage is one in which both the husband and wife are uniquely themselves. And as they seek to live in submission to one another with their uniqueness intact, they discover that in some awesome way their uniqueness either complements their spouse's or that their uniqueness is a part of God's design to help their spouse grow into greater Christlikeness.

A healthy church, like a healthy marriage, is a people on mission with Christ recognizing that our differences are significant to the kingdom and the reality is that we don't have to stifle our quirkiness; we just look to the cross together because we realize we cannot grow in Christ apart from the church. Growth demands change. Change creates conflict. Conflict produces tension. Tension exists to be leveraged.

The cross is the greatest source of tension the world has ever known. But on it God leveraged great tension, the reality of humanity's sin and gift of His grace, to create an alternative reality known as the kingdom of God that could be produced only by the conflict that is the crucifixion.

DISCUSSION QUESTIONS

How does the imagery of a marriage help us in understanding the church and community?

Why do we associate community with people who like one another? Why do we tend to gravitate toward those who are like us? How should the church be different?

Respond to the statement, "Community lies on the other side of conflict." Do you agree? Why or why not?

How do you feel about the statement, "You cannot grow in Christ apart from the church?" How does that impact how we understand conflict?

03

DESPAIR vs. HOPE

Video Transcript—Stanley Hauerwas

Despair is a sin. If you're a Christian, you are committed to hope because God requires it. *Faith, hope,* and *love.* So my general sense is that God in this time is making us leaner and meaner as Christians. And that's a sign of great hope. Simply

VIDEO TRANSCRIPT

because we're free. We might as well have some fun in what we're doing. I mean I think of being a Christian as being—what an interesting, fun thing God has given us: we don't have to make the world work.

Duke University has allegedly a Methodist background, but it's a very secular university. And I like that a lot. I mean I'm not running this place, so I don't have to try to figure out how to make it work. I'm free. I don't have to think about what is the necessary ideology to sustain Duke University. I'm just trying to say what I think being a Christian is about and the intellectual challenges of that in the world in which we find ourselves. Hopefully, other people will find that interesting because we don't say just what everyone in the university is saying today.

So I'm a very hopeful guy. I think this is a time that God is finally helping us as Christians get over what is called Christendom—namely, when we thought we were in control of the world. It's terrific. We're discovering we're going to be forced to learn how to live by our wits. When you have power, it dulls the mind, and it dulls the intellect. We're learning what it means to live without power. We may learn to live wittily again. When you're not in control then you have to know those who are in control better than they know themselves in order to survive. That's great. We can do that now in a way that I think is quite promising.

DISCUSSION QUESTIONS

Do you agree that "despair is a sin?"
Why or why not?

How is the church changing? Why is it changing? What does it mean for the church to become "leaner and meaner?"

Respond to this statement by Hauerwas: "We don't have to make the world work." What does he mean? What does that mean for us?

What is Christendom? Why do we need to get over it? What is next for us?

Despair is a sin.

STANLEY HAUERWAS

Hope is the refusal to accept the reading of reality which is the majority opinion; and one does that only at great political and existential risk. On the other hand, hope is subversive, for it limits the grandiose pretensions of the present, daring to announce that the present to which we have all made commitments is now called into question.[5]

WALTER BRUEGGEMANN

[5] Walter Brueggemann, *The Prophetic Imagination* (Minneapolis, MN: Fortress Press 2001), 67.

I live in a small factory town in northeast Ohio. Given the U.S.'s current economic climate, you can probably sense where this story is going. The factories shut down and people lost their jobs. Now the community is experiencing this pervasive feeling that the town's best days have passed. The people are busy securing whatever money they have left and defending their territory (i.e., their homes). In short, they are in survival mode.

COMMENTARY

The church where I serve has been a part of this community for almost 125 years. It has witnessed a lot as it has shared over a century's worth of history. More than simply witnessing the life of the community, the church has been the incarnational hands and feet of Jesus, which means that just as Jesus took on our flesh and lived among us so also this little band of Jesus followers cannot help but take on some of the pain and sadness of the town as the church lives out the incarnational journey of Jesus.

Hauerwas begins this video clip by declaring that "despair is a sin." His language sounds very strong, but I think he's right and the Scriptures back him up. Let's consider this idea of despair for a moment. When God calls Joshua and his crew to enter the Promised Land, he encourages them with these words: "Have I not commanded you? Be strong and courageous. Do not be terrified; do not be discouraged, for the LORD your God will be with you wherever you go" (Josh. 1:9). That same language has already been used two times prior in verses 6 and 7. God has a mission for Joshua to accomplish, and it is imperative for Joshua to understand that he not be in despair, not be discouraged, nor live in fear about that mission because God is with him.

This language is present throughout the Scriptures. God shows up or gives a directive, in some ways harkening the listener(s) back to the words he gave to Joshua. Look at the following passages to see some of the similarities:

So do not fear, for I am with you; do not be dismayed, for I am your God. I will strengthen you and help you; I will uphold you with my righteous right hand. (Isa. 41:10)

God is our refuge and strength, an ever-present help in trouble. Therefore we will not fear, though the earth give way and the mountains fall into the heart of the sea, though its waters roar and foam and the mountains quake with their surging. (Ps. 46:1-3)

Your Father knows what you need before you ask him. So do not worry, saying "What shall we eat?" or "What shall we drink" or "What shall we wear?" For the pagans run after all these things, and your heavenly Father knows that you need them. But seek first his kingdom and his righteousness, and all these things will be given to you as well. Therefore do not worry about tomorrow, for tomorrow will worry about itself. Each day has enough trouble of its own. (Matt. 6:8b, 31-34)

For we do not have a high priest who is unable to sympathize with our weaknesses, but we have one who has been tempted in every way, just as we are—yet was without sin. Let us then approach the throne of grace with confidence, so that we may receive mercy and find grace to help in our time of need. (Heb. 4:15-16)

The above verses are just a few examples of the overwhelming volume of scripture on this particular area. God does not want his people to be in despair. He does not want his people to live in fear of the world, to live dejected lives, to be unable to connect with him, or to lack boldness, power and zeal.

So when the Apostle Paul writes to the church in Thessalonica, he challenges them to have this attitude even when they face the death of loved ones: "Brothers, we do not want you to be ignorant about those who fall asleep, or to grieve like the rest of men, who have no hope" (1 Thess. 4:13). While the world grieves without hope or direction, followers of Jesus grieve very differently. Pain is not removed, but what we do with that pain is quite different—at least it should be.

What if the opposite of faith is not disbelief? After all, the father who came to Jesus with his demon-possessed son cried out, "'I do believe; help me overcome my unbelief'" (Mark 9:24). What if the opposite of faith is despair? What if despair negates our faith? If faith is the public sign of that which we hope for (Heb. 11:1) and call the world to, then might despair stand in the way of the grand mission of God to which we're called?

It seems that we feel despair when we feel powerless and feel like our best days are behind us, when our lives and the things we encounter (be it tragedy or frustration) do not connect to some larger story. (Keep in mind that a postmodern climate seeks to get people to buy into the idea that there is no larger story, or meta-narrative, and we all just simply need to live out our own individual story.)

The reality for the follower of Jesus is that, as Hauerwas says, we do not need to make the world work. This lie from Christendom has led to more despair than hope. When people die unexpectedly, we don't have to act like we understand or know why. When economies tank, we don't have to have all the answers. You see, when we assume we need to have all the answers and need to eliminate all the mystery in the world, we crucify hope, never experiencing the kingdom reality that is faith.

C. S. Lewis captures the tension of despair and hope in his book *The Problem of Pain.* In it he writes, "Pain removes the veil; it plants the flag of truth within the fortress of the rebel soul."[6] Pain and suffering are the great equalizers of humanity. If you haven't suffered, you will. What we do with this frustration we call pain is the "flag of truth" of which Lewis speaks. Pain and suffering will reveal if we're a people of despair or a people of hope.

So in these times when God is making us "leaner and meaner as Christians," as Hauerwas puts it, how will we respond? Our response offers the world a glimpse of who our God is— either the God of Abraham, Isaac, and Jacob made known to us in Jesus, or ourselves and our most recent quest for transcendence via the newest product on the market.

Pain can focus us and deepen our longing for the grand restoration of this world (no more weeping, no more pain, no more violence) by God's grace and power. Or, pain can call out our high levels of narcissism when we think it's up to us to run the world and to make it make sense. That treadmill exhausts anyone.

If we allow ourselves to get over the quest for power and begin to embrace and live out the adventure that is salvation, the church could witness unprecedented growth in this new age. Where power has dulled down our intellects and imaginations,

[6] C. S. Lewis, *The Problem of Pain* (New York: Harper One 2001), 93-94.

we can "wittily" learn to live and have great hope not in church strategies or gimmicks but in the all-surpassing hope and love of God.

Even in my northeast Ohio piece of the map, it is a sin to believe our best days are behind us. Our jobs should never be our identity. Neither should our families. Nor should the amount of money in our checking account. In the end, our identity as followers of Jesus is in the great adventurer named Jesus and in following him. In that journey we take bold, ridiculous, passionate risk because as the Apostle Paul said to the church in Rome:

> If God is for us, who can be against us? Who shall separate us from the love of Christ? Shall trouble or hardship or persecution or famine or nakedness or danger or sword? No, in all these things we are more than conquerors through him who loved us. For I am convinced that neither death nor life, neither angels nor demons, neither the present nor the future, nor any powers, neither height nor depth, nor anything else in all creation, will be able to separate us from the love of God that is in Christ Jesus our Lord. (Rom. 8:31b, 35, 37-39)

As we relinquish the power and need to make the world work we begin to see the world more objectively and tackle the issues God cares about. Then faith moves from passive noun (concepts) to active verb (risks), and we realize that we could never know those in power and the pertinent issues well enough if we were still in the ring jockeying for power.

DISCUSSION QUESTIONS

Where have you felt fear in your life? Where have you taken great risk? How are the two related?

Do you agree that the opposite of faith is not disbelief but despair? Why or why not? Reflect on Mark 4:35-41 as you respond to this question.

How do you feel about the statement, "If you haven't suffered, you will?" Does it make you uneasy? Why or why not?

04

CONTEMPORARY WORSHIP
vs. WORSHIP

Video Transcript—Stanley Hauerwas

I think that one of the things that bothers me the most about so much of contemporary Christian worship is it's ugly. It's just ugly. I don't get why it attracts people. I don't get it. And I worry, I worry about souls that, I know this sounds terrible, that are so superficial they're attracted to that form of worship. I mean I can't imagine.

VIDEO TRANSCRIPT

You can only be taken in by it if you want to avoid recognizing the terror and the unbelievable tragedy that surrounds us. I mean, we live in an ugly world, and, I don't mean that it's going to be that that means you need a lot of Rembrandt hanging around and that sort of thing. I think of a Quaker meetinghouse as extraordinarily beautiful. Just the simplicity of it. And the people are beautiful. It's that that seems to me we really need to work very hard to articulate for ourselves.

One of the things I don't like about the church growth movement is how it creates a very homogenous congregation of approximately the same ages. And I think that has to do with the worship being fundamentally a form of entertainment in which the congregation doesn't do any work. I mean liturgy is the work of the people. The Greeks meant, "oh, you're digging a trench for water that you do to gather." That was liturgy. When the congregation is not part of the work of prayer that's at the heart of the liturgical life, then something has desperately gone wrong.

When you have to keep coming up with variety in the name of attracting new people all the time, what a terrible treadmill that must be to be on. And when the sermon is primarily thought just to keep you entertained rather than you to receive it as part of the work of the congregation, then, if you compete with television, television in the end is going to win because it's so good at what it does. The liturgy has got to be a real alternative to that. And if it is, it will be in a certain sense more entertaining than television because it will pull us out of our everyday presumptions that we know what it is we need and want.

DISCUSSION QUESTIONS

Respond to Hauerwas's claim that "so much of contemporary Christian worship is ugly." How does this statement make you feel? Does it affirm or contradict your view? How?

Do you feel worship has become "a form of entertainment?" If so, how did we get here? If not, why might Hauerwas feel this way?

How can we begin to do "the work of the people" rather than simply consuming worship and expecting to be entertained? How might more participation in the liturgy, the prayers, change the direction of our services?

"If [we] compete with television, television in the end is going to win because it's so good at what it does." Respond to that statement. Do you think Hauerwas is correct? Why or why not?

[Liturgy] will pull us out of our everyday presumptions that we know what it is we need and want.

STANLEY HAUERWAS

The significance of the historical orientation of biblical worship is this: Worship re-creates and thus re-presents the historical event. In this way worship proclaims the meaning of the original event and confronts worshipers with the claim of God over their lives. Therefore, the overriding concern of worship is not simply the reenactment of the event, but a personal meeting with God. On one side, the emphasis is on God who has acted; on the other side, the emphasis is on humans responding. In this way something happens in worship: God and his people meet. Worship is not simply going through the motions of ceremony. It becomes the visible and tangible meeting of God through the signs and symbols of his presence.[7]

ROBERT WEBBER

[7] Robert Webber, *Worship Old & New* (Grand Rapids, MI: Zondervan 1994), 25.

Sometimes I'm more comfortable with the idea of a distant (deist) God than a relational (theist) God. I like to study God and talk about him, but the personal, intimate, relational side can sometimes make me feel very unsettled.

COMMENTARY But the God of Abraham, Isaac and Jacob, the God who called Moses and Joshua, the God who saw the runt of the family and made him King David, the God who called David's son Solomon to the throne, the God who journeyed with his people from times of great power to times of tragic exile, the God of the great period of silence in the inter-testamental period, and the God revealed to us in Jesus, crucified, resurrected, and coming again is not a distant, deistic God. He is relational. My standards for following God need to be adjusted around that truth. One of the defining truths of Christianity is that God is in relationship with us whether we like to believe it or not.

Here is the odd thing. As I struggle to leave behind my deistic sentiments and embrace the one true, relational God, I notice friction between other believers and me. It seems that in my journey for the real, relational God, I cannot experience his existence without embracing the raw, untamed reality of who he is. The friction occurs because as I head from deist to theist many other believers are on this Enlightenment understanding of the faith that moves them from a relational God to a deistic God with a deistic moral code meant to make good, moral people, never mind some of the most boring followers of Jesus you'll ever meet.[8]

I think this is what Hauerwas is up to when he starts the video with the little quip, "So much of contemporary Christian worship is ugly." Its ugliness comes in that it exists divorced from the reality of the world you and I know. While there is horrific violence and terror in the world, much of contemporary Christian worship exists almost inside a vacuum seeking to conjure up the next emotional high for those sucked into its attractional orbit.

Its ugliness also comes in that the beauty and variety that is the body of Christ gets reduced down to a homogenous group of people who may be of the same age, sharing a space rather than a history, and passively consuming "religious goods." These people are never challenged to greatness or offered the chance to bring something to the gathering.

Several years ago the World Bank wanted to get a grasp of how countries outside the West understood poverty. The feeling was that Westerners, especially Americans, had too materialistic

[8] The Enlightenment is the era in Western philosophy, intellectual, scientific and cultural life, developed during the 18th century, in which reason was advocated as the primary source for legitimacy and authority. The Enlightenment sought to rid humanity of religious and traditional claims. The Enlightenment, with its elevation of reason, created the concept of the deistic, distant God. Religion became a tool for creating good, moral people. Any supernatural relational attributes of Christianity were downplayed or eliminated.

a definition of poverty. What the World Bank discovered was that from nations around the world a common thread was seen in understandings of poverty. Poverty seemed to be how a people felt and lived when they were unable to make a unique contribution to the betterment of society.[9]

This is what Hauerwas is getting to when he discusses the ugliness of contemporary Christian worship. People are not empowered or challenged but are left impoverished, denied to make their unique contribution to worship. Instead of attracting and creating deep souls able to withstand the challenges of life and faith, we create superficial people who need their next fix. All along, the church is more and more impoverished. Worship services get reduced down to a form of entertainment. And, as Hauerwas says, if we compete with television, "television will win in the end."

This conversation reminds me of the story of Jesus's encounter with the woman at the well—where a chance meeting turns into a remarkable story of grace, forgiveness, and the meaning of worship. The woman is a Samaritan (despised because of her ethnicity and even lower because of her gender). She is out in the middle of the day, which is odd. And, on top of that, she is engaging Jesus in a conversation (and vice versa). This Samaritan woman recognizes that Jesus must be some sort of

[9] For more on this conversation check out *When Helping Hurts: Alleviating Poverty Without Hurting the Poor... and Yourself* by Brian Fikkert and Steve Corbett. It shows how the conversation of poverty goes far beyond materialistic fixes and includes deeper issues of wholeness, restoration, and even worship.

prophet; she begins to lament about how her people used to worship and how the Jews claim that worship can occur only in the temple at Jerusalem. Jesus's response is powerful for his day—and our own:

> Jesus declared, "Believe me, woman, a time is coming when you will worship the Father neither on this mountain nor in Jerusalem. You Samaritans worship what you do not know; we worship what we do know, for salvation is from the Jews. Yet a time is coming and has now come when the true worshipers will worship the Father in spirit and truth, for they are the kind of worshipers the Father seeks. God is spirit, and his worshipers must worship in spirit and in truth." (John 4:21-24)

At that well, the Samaritan woman was talking to her greatest hope, the bearer of salvation and the embodiment of God. He was not in a temple; he was not a ritualistic system. He was a human. He was present. He spoke deep words of truth to her. He saw her for who she really was.

Spirit and truth develop an interesting tension. John's gospel reads, "For the law was given through Moses; grace and truth came through Jesus Christ" (1:17). God declares the following through the prophet Jeremiah about the new covenant he will make: "'This is the covenant I will make with the house of Israel after that time,' declares the LORD. 'I will put my law in their minds and write it on their hearts. I will be their God, and they will be my people'" (Jer. 31:33).

The law was given to Moses as a standard for the people God had called. Jesus fulfilled that standard and through him came a new era of truth and grace. The era is not new as in brand new but new as in fresh. Through Jesus the story is being retold again. We are a people who are spiritual and human. We are to live lives of grace and truth. To worship God in Spirit and in truth is to recognize that God is Spirit but that he is also tangibly true in the people sitting around us.

The downfall of evangelicalism in America in recent years is that it has stressed so much the personal side of the faith that it's become almost private. Evangelicalism has treated corporate worship, the entire church even, like it's simply an add-on at the end of God's plan. But the mission of God all throughout Scripture is God seeking to create a people for himself. God desires community outside of himself. God knows no other reality besides a communal reality. The mystery of the trinity is that this mystical oneness exists in three communally distinct parts.

The ugliness of much of contemporary Christian worship is that we totally miss what the community of faith is meant to be in the life of a believer. When the body gathers, the believers tangibly live out what it means to die to self on behalf of Christ.

I submit to the community and relinquish my rights to that community. I submit my plans, my desire for entertainment, my personal agendas and join the work, the mission, the liturgy (work of the people)[10] of the community with whom I'm on mission.

So maybe the deepening of evangelical churches and our quest for the relational God all come in the type of liturgy the church uses—the amount and type of work we're doing together. Is your church employing an attractive, constantly changing liturgy that is continuously in flux depending on where the cultural winds blow? Or is your church anchoring people in the story of God by allowing them to participate in the reading of Scripture, challenging its members to go beyond mere therapeutic (oftentimes narcissistic) prayer to prayers of hope and justice, singing praise worthy of a king, and receiving the message or sermon as a word and directive from the Lord?

How will you know? You'll know when you stop judging worship the way most contemporary Christian services have (i.e., bucks and behinds and how did it speak to me?). And you'll know when you start asking, "What did I contribute to the work of the people?" Church is not a show to watch on Sunday—it is a people on mission making known the tangible reality of the kingdom of a relational God.

[10] Liturgy comes from the Greek word *leitourgia* that literally means "work of the people."

DISCUSSION QUESTIONS

How do Western Christians tend to be "confessing theists but walking deists?" Why does faith so quickly become concepts and beliefs?

Do you agree with the statement that "people [in many forms of contemporary Christian worship] are left impoverished [and] denied to make their unique contribution?"
Why or why not?

What is church? What does it mean for it to be the body of Christ?

05

THE SYSTEM VS. THE KINGDOM

Video Transcript—Stanley Hauerwas

Is there any training we can do to embrace death so we can live better?

VIDEO TRANSCRIPT

I think prayer is really a part of the training that's involved. I think going to church is a good place. I think worshiping God with other people is absolutely essential to learning to live as a Christian. This is not work that can be done by yourself. It can only be done in a community through which you are made part of an ongoing history that you don't get to make up. Too often American Christians, I think, think they get to make Christianity up. But it's received. You get American Christians oftentimes who think of themselves as very conservative saying things like, "I believe Jesus is Lord, but that's just my personal opinion." What produced that peculiar speech act? What produced that peculiar speech act is the distinction between "being a Christian that's kind of my private life, but then I have this public stuff."

Tolerance kills us. I don't have any private life as a Christian. It's all public. That Jesus is Lord is going to make my life quite dysfunctional in relationship to a good deal of American practice. Being a Christian should just scare us. It's like on Sunday we need to rush to gather for protection. It's like, "Oh, I'm not crazy!" because that we believe that God was in Christ reconciling the world is craziness. It's going to make your life really weird. You just need to get together on Sunday to be pulled back into the reality of God's kingdom, which I believe we do, I mean it's there in baptism and the proclamation of the Word and the Eucharistic celebration.

DISCUSSION QUESTIONS

What does Hauerwas mean when he says, "Too often American Christians think they get to make Christianity up?" Do you agree? Why or why not?

Do you believe that following Jesus will make my life "dysfunctional" to most Americans? What does this mean and look like? How can we be different and still function in society? Are there specific rules to which we should all subscribe?

Discuss the craziness of the biblical announcement that God is in Christ reconciling the world. How is this crazy?

In what ways does the church pull us into the "reality of God's kingdom" (or in what ways should it)? What does this mean?

Too often American Christians, I think,
think they get to make Christianity up.
But it's received.

STANLEY HAUERWAS

As soon as we say Christian theology we also say church theology. To be a follower of Christ has meant from the beginning to join the community of disciples he draws together around himself. Christ himself promised to make himself known especially where people were gathered together in his name. The bible was not written for and about isolated individuals; it was written for and about a community of people… You can be a Christian theologian only as you do your work in conversation with other Christians in the Christian community, as together with them you seek to learn what God is doing and what God also has for you to do in the world outside the church.[11]

SHIRLEY GUTHRIE

[11] Shirley Guthrie, *Christian Doctrine* (Louisville, KY: Westminster John Knox Press 1994), 15.

Some time ago I was asked to speak to a group of teenagers at a denominational rally. During one of my talks, I saw a young man in the front row texting away. I noticed because he never made eye contact with me and his phone kept vibrating again and again. After the message I went over to the young man and politely asked, "Why were you texting so much while I was talking?" His response surprised me: "I'm sorry. I was just breaking up with my girlfriend." That was bad enough. Imagine my horror when I realized that his girlfriend, now ex-girlfriend, had been sitting in the row right behind him the whole time.

COMMENTARY

I could easily dismiss this young man's behavior as typical for someone his age, but I think there's more to it than that. We live in a time and culture in which the public sphere has become an extension of the private. We exist in our own world, quite literally. We join a community of faith on a Sunday morning and leave judging the entire service not by what we contributed but by what it did, or didn't, do for us. "The worship was slow." "The sermon dragged on." "The people didn't all greet me." We go to church on Sunday without ever really showing up.

Hauerwas comments, "Too often, American Christians think they get to make Christianity up. But it's received." Too often we think we get to craft our life and find the systems, people, and places that serve us best. Then, we squeeze Jesus into whatever time is left. Too many well-intentioned, good, moral people have not recognized the supremacy and lordship of Jesus Christ. Too many Americans are drinking a punch that has been laced with the lie of compartmentalization, existing like walking iPads: there's my "work me," my "school me," my "family me," and my "church me."

But we were designed as integrated, holistic beings. Spiritual is tied to emotional, emotional to physical, physical to mental, and so on. Anything that seeks to compartmentalize these different areas of our life actually robs us of our humanity. For a Christian, as Hauerwas argues, there is no "private life." And as the earlier video on contemporary Christian worship showed, we are made to be with a community of believers with whom we share a story, a common history.

Our faith communities should make this bold declaration to the world, which Hauerwas talks about: "We believe God was in Christ reconciling the world." That reality for followers of Jesus is crazy talk to the rest of the world. It is not logical to have hope of resurrection or afterlife. But somewhere right about where logic and reason stop, faith picks up and makes the bold assertion and profound truth that there is more—much more.

When the Apostle Paul wrote to the church in Corinth, he felt this tension. Paul lived in the tension between his Jewish history and the Greeks' rationalistic worldview. When it came to the message of the cross he wrote, "For the message of the cross is foolishness to those who are perishing, but to us who are being saved it is the power of God" (1 Cor. 1:18).

The Jews demanded signs, Paul goes on to say, and the Greeks demanded wisdom. But the only thing followers of Jesus have is the cross. The Jews denied Christ's divinity, asserting that a convict was executed. The Greeks denied that any true religion would assert the foolish idea that a god would take flesh (which was considered the root of evil by some Greek groups). Both sides rejected the message but, either way, Christ was more than a man and more than a bodiless mind/spirit. Much like today, these two groups were seeking to compartmentalize the message of the cross. They took their cues from their cultural context first and sought to make Christianity fit that mold. But to be a follower of Jesus means that my cues come, first and foremost, from God—then I see how everything else fits.

C. S. Lewis once wrote, "I believe in Christianity as I believe that the sun has risen, not only because I see it, but because by it I see everything else."[12] This is the heart of Christianity and the heart of the Christian. The true follower of Jesus does not see the world in the same way as an unbeliever. The believer sees the world through the eyes of God, and that vision is made tangible by the community of disciples with whom they are on mission.

[12] C. S. Lewis, *The Weight of Glory* (New York: Harper One 2001), 140.

While the world says, "believe what you want but make sure it remains a private preference," we proclaim the exact opposite. Tolerating this worldview kills the mission of God in God's church—following Jesus is not meant to make my life safe, secure, comfortable, or more tolerable to a majority of Americans. It definitely won't compartmentalize down to a nice, cozy pocket! In the same way, Jesus is larger than a political affiliation, so my allegiance to him should be greater than my allegiance to a political party. Following Jesus, as Hauerwas states, "is going to make my life dysfunctional to most Americans."

The church is the people of God on mission. Our Sunday gatherings should be times when we all get together and check in with one another. This mission of reconciling the world back to God through Christ is crazy. It simply doesn't make sense. But we are not a pragmatic people who look for more effective ways to live. For two millennia it's been the same thing: the gospel remains Jesus Christ crucified, resurrected, and coming again.

We tell the story over and over to one another because we're sharing a history together—a history that allows each member of the community to truly be who he or she is since community lies on the other side of conflict. In a world of intense ugliness and despair, we model the alternative of hope rooted in the providence of God. And because of that hope our worship is about actively contributing to the one true, relational God—not simply getting our religious fix on Sunday mornings.

Following Jesus, as Hauerwas so eloquently mentions, should "scare us." It is the most demanding call one could ever heed: after all, the one we follow was killed for his mission! Yet somehow we cannot say no because it is the one true adventure we'll ever be offered. It's not about merely getting to heaven. It's about being a people fully alive and fully present in a communication-obsessed yet somehow still disengaged world.

The church by its very witness models an alternative. And as we enjoy God more than ever before, love each other more deeply than ever before, and care better for our communities than ever before, we make the kingdom tangible. No compartmentalized, compromised, accommodated witness has ever been able to do that or ever will. Welcome to a band of ragamuffin disciples who are in need of a Sunday asylum. Welcome, my friends, to the adventure that is the church.

DISCUSSION QUESTIONS

How has the faith become private? What is the difference between personal and private? Why does this matter?

How do you feel about the myth of "compartmentalization?" Is it a myth? What does it do to us as humans to see ourselves like iPads?

Respond to the C. S. Lewis quote, "I believe in Christianity as I believe that the sun has risen, not only because I see it, but because by it I see everything else."

Does following Jesus ever scare you? Why or why not?

BONUS MATERIAL

The following three video transcripts are from additional time with Stanley Hauerwas. Feel free to use this material however you like.

CHURCH GROWTH VS. REPETITION

I've always said church growth churches will be successful for fifteen to twenty years. But then how do you reproduce yourself the next generation? The Catholic Church is very good at being slow and waitin' it out. And I'm for waitin' it out. I mean it takes great patience and stamina and a lot of energy to do the same thing all the time, and I'm for doing the same thing all the time. I want, when I go to worship God, I want to know that prayer is going to be said: "On the night he was betrayed, he took bread."

And so I'm for repetition. And it's not like you're just keeping things the same because everything around you is changing, so what you're doing is different though it is the same.

AMERICAN TIME VS.CHURCH TIME

Let's say a church brought you and said, we're going to pay you money to recapture liturgy in our church— you have carte blanche, you can do whatever you want or force us to do whatever you want. What would you do?

I would make sure you never observe Mother's Day, and Thanksgiving and July 4th is out too. You would be put on a different time—church time. You would have to have your life determined by church time and why it is that the year doesn't start with New Year's but with Advent and why it climaxes at Pentecost. That would be a way of reconstructing. For helping you get a sense of how it is you're not living in the same time as people who are living in American time. So, it's a very small thing.

Why are our imaginations so dull?

Because that's the way you sell products. Capitalism dulls the imagination in order to make sure you're the kind of person who thinks they've had a choice when they think they have to choose between a Sony and a Panasonic—it's not much of a choice.

THE GIFT OF OFFENSIVE SPEECH

I'm a very conventional guy. I don't think of myself as peculiarly radical though many people seem to find what I say and write more challenging than I do.

Why do you think that is? Why do they label you? What is it you challenge? What do you poke a stick at?

I guess I seem to have the ability to say what I think Christians should say—offensively. And you know that's a gift God gave me, and I also say it with a sense of humor. I don't try necessarily to do that, but it seems to happen and that makes people think twice about it. Because I do have good humor about where we are and where I think we're gonna be going.

NOTES

NOTES

NOTES

PSALMIST'S CRY
Scripts for Embracing Lament
Walter Brueggemann with Steve Frost

As Christians, we've lost the danger of the gospel—the part where we give up control and allow God's mystery to unfold in our lives—and in doing so, we've lost the depth of its goodness. In this 5-week study, discover the fullness of God when we allow our lives to become about him healing us and not about us controlling or managing our way through life.

DVD+Book	978-0-8341-2594-0	**$39.99**
Book	978-0-8341-2593-3	**$12.99**

To order go to thehousestudio.com

ECONOMY OF LOVE
Creating a Community of Enough

A Resource of Relational Tithe

Video Sessions with Shane Claiborne

In this five-week study, unpack what the patterns of God's kingdom look like compared to the patterns of our world. What is the value of enough, and how do we become more like the God who is close to the poor, the hungry, the meek, and the merciful?

Economy of Love will challenge individuals to join in community, journeying together as they begin to consider a new standard of living—a personal economic threshold oriented not around the size of a monthly paycheck, but around the value of enough.

To order go to thehousestudio.com